This notebook belongs to:

____

Accountant Life Publishing

Made in the USA
Las Vegas, NV
12 November 2023

80661692R00066